small siren

small siren

Poems by Alexandra Mattraw

The Cultural Society
Brooklyn MMXVIII

small siren
ISBN 978-0-9994912-2-5
© 2018 by Alexandra Mattraw
all rights reserved

Second edition

For permission to reprint more than a few lines from this book
or for other inquiry, please write to The Cultural Society:
culturalsociety.org
publisher@culturalsociety.org

Contents

at the yield point : in the way of harbors

Acknowledgements

A fraction of the poems in this book have also appeared in various chapbooks, including *in the way of harbors* (2013) and *flood psalm* (2017), both by Dancing Girl Press, as well as *these threads a sound* (Beard of Bees, 2013) and *Projection* (Achiote Press, 2010). Many of those poems have since been revised to meet the vision of this book. Poems have also been featured in the following journals, anthologies, and art shows:

1913: A Journal of Forms, alice blue review, American Letters & Commentary, Brooklyn's BWAC (Brooklyn Waterfront Artist's Coalition) Black & White Art Show, The Cultural Society, Denver Quarterly, Fourteen Hills, Monday Night, RealPoetik, Thethepoetry, Remembering the Days that Breathed Pink (anthology) from Quaci Press, *Seneca Review, Shampoo, Switchback, Verse, VOLT*, and *Word For/Word*

these threads : a sound

The yield stage may be in fact a destruction of the record of the past life of the material.

Her raw mouth removed from not

knowing : A fjörd, a black beach, rock spines

thickened or thinned by ocean : Songs

she rubs, cliff-rims : Gray-green rounds pressed

leaf-shaped to wet street : Asphalt

rain : Sour hummed reach of her metal

chambered microphone : When is a voice

a piano : Hunched back gilded tendons,

sinews : Strings woven by what can't tie

so many circles make a song : Transitions

cut audiences : Red flesh chaps

her tongue to lip : Gluts red clapboards

under sun, under lamplit swings yellow fielded

: Repetition needs to believe : believe : a heresy :

to shape / hillside distance / a hickory smell / in your exhale / we must cross / the swollen water

Muse Rituals

: I arrange the table according to hunger : A box
inside a lake inside a piggy jar : I can promise
little : Each glass holds
a meadow inside it : Tulips aren't
punctual or candy pink, but a green click behind
eyelids : Rain lull : Apple true and listing, you look
for those names : There will be rain, but drops
feather wind blown glass : Deer as only a place
for twigs snapping underfoot : Jagged pine tops to question
the placement of stars : You speak grass : Thistle the arc
stream of a water hose caught midstorm : You contest
a hill's M-shape : A venn diagram you call *loss* :
A sky of eggshells : We'll feel discomfort : A crack
in my wooden table : The lamp of your hair :

separately late winter / now river / bridges a fell tree / warped in the middle / I scuttle a moss log

Aught, unknowing, a summer

A palace rendered from field weeds : Tidal
fringe : Between quiet foot imprints : Mud
routings : Not the wooden
toys children polish : I woke, walked,
revived by sepals' violet : Wind chides : Sounds
I reasoned with a dirt road, in the sense of
already being a place : Phrases
blemish, spoken to no one : To reeds :
Allowances : I lean in, votive,
in the going, in streetside raw
agate : I denounce red and green
codes : Fumes shine street clocks :
Church domes mediate diesel : Fog arches
the marble train station : I chase myself :

mosquito nets / heavy swarming, of falling / I am terrified / we wash our hands / in river turns

Eros

: A sea settles a dock of breath

across summer : Invisible chimney heat

rises in unused bricks : Thickening neat

New England hours : Our mouths arrest

light : Threshing dune grass sweats

your pale blouse blown out : Dressed in cloud

crease and evening *Does all such water allow*

addiction? Or, is this where need begins?

In wave-crest you construct a piano : Of ivory caps you demand

message : Wind performs seaweed strings, beer bottles green

we collect to whisper fog : Clam shells breach flesh : Sand

opens : Twin crab husks gutting voice lap

: Our white beach umbrella pitched by land-lean :

A dress flipped back to sea we'll never reach :

we fight in the car / as usual, following / too close, speed / muting the radio / sky blare smacks

Bridge Demolition

Again, we awake to chatter of teeth hitting a concrete
heartbeat : Heard
within my ear : A tractor begets its face of garden
trowels to dig the rusted : out : Wet birdleaf plumes
brandy cedar and shavings scent my hands : All bodies torn
from water : Rumbles thunder our words pushed
back : Punched
sheetrock chalks the river in chunks : Islands splatter, but then
what? No longer a path, pine needles brown ants
I count to know a future : Even means life,
odd, the other : A nod rips *yes*
and hammers agate *no* no longer : Bridge
enamel now teeth fillings all knocked out : A pulse
mouths sounds
and what heats loosens to make us : Sand falls back
to sand : Again, what returns
in metal shudders to finish
us is smaller,
more exact.

at mountain edge / the road shuffles us / loose like pocket change / *look!* you smile, pointing

Inside the Whale

You see yourself : a photograph inside
a mirror : You want to record silence
but can't find it inside : water
or sunlight where whales sing
the same a year after returning
to the same sea : He'll kill himself
they said but you think : chance songs
remembered : when your father axed
the piano and made lyrics
from splinters : sickled keys : You voice
or film over mother's milk : what grew
before you could speak :
blood : air : breath :
torsion's lifting—

four Llamas chime the parking lot / where we arrive / a sky of black fur / & small bells whirl

A Desert Sounds

You beckon from the tent : Canyon slot rock walls redden
all that becomes nearer : Each exposure a history :
Sudden rain sketches veined patterns in the thick of it
: Sand sprawl wind written only for sound : Now a veil,
a wet sieve grows downward unrelenting : Pinion pines well
up to meet them : You ask my ring size : Creaks twist
a juniper bone claw upturned to demand naming : I argue but cacti
bloom saffron one day a year : Call them pear, hedgehog, or
fishhook as really a voice on my tongue : Not their yellow cupped
petals but : the space around them : Is it your or our :
Cottonwoods resemble wind : funneled sea rush, riverbed crickets
brush foxtails : Leg-spine stubble chirps in unknown glow
: White t-shirts flag snap the hitching post dry : Denuded,
iron heavy skin sweats into air : Tree stumps
anchor rocks, sound what is closer :

here is laughter I promise you / backyard lemon tree / trowels out sour / pigeon coo / pigeon loam

Casino Proposals

Upsweep sun stubble : Pardon : language that turns back

on itself : From inside, gamble : red categories laid open : Draw

a ring around tabling : Tobacco heavy, the word

notch a checkered truss : assembly : You don't trust such

enterprise so you reverse : letters and make capital

good time : Dinner fiddleheads : gravy swallowed whiskey

spells good spill and gets some : Nickel dealers shine

crescents into lull slots : Bacchus swivel ritual of one

to two then wet : sheets, nothing : Pine sticky, how

can any symbol manage itself : A trophy life, but the sky

will branch bluer : with no stars to barnacle : I respond

to such circles : but you wed me to heresy : Lemon rind thick

between tongue and cherry lap : Test taste the role reversal

en masse : Lit wishes born with one quarter and a half wick :

before returning home / you buy me earrings that dangle / a red stone perching / you call *canary*

The Fray

Helicopters swing static : treetops I imagine he is
redwood : Bones break : All canopies fall he says
tossing back the river : brown into his throat
: where backyard ash pits darken stasis :
Imagine her palm that grows tinier
in mine : Her face still wet with trust
only water has for sky : certain to pick it up
again : into daylight : feathers born to swarm
listening : I press my ear to hers : All sirens
are there : circling nightfall once : none :
once : no one : Inside her tide rushes to pulse
then hushes mine : To beat back :
Not unlike this slow wind
shield : our woman
arms born

our eyes mesh into linen reams / wet bird-leaf flickers a ruse / a moan I make / accidently in sleep

Muse Rituals

: Rain from us the world : Call us walls
invisible : In her, a brick of music : A mouth
she runs to roof : In us, protest a figure's
rain : A pail hides her field's strain :
Gossamer whips with iris : Carp shouts trout
with sky : She rains her own destroyer,
I : You destroy, raining, I : Sheets awake skirts
raining : Pleats rain linen sleep : Rain draped
streets I sour : Shingled rain knows speaking
: With unknown rain shipped oceans : She reels
afloat my river : Treading rain temporal : Wash
our disarranged : Soaked rain holds
withdrawal : Lose rain in assemble : Grief
pales my window : Sketched so *we* is vain :

Inside the Construction

The yield point refers to the load at which solid material that is being stretched begins to flow or change shape permanently.

Summary Between

Each pasture clots a day's naming. We stop field center, but the green world sweats, thickens like hair. The way an orange unpeels itself in such heat. All bruised skin wants to give way in the manner of water. We share corner store bread. Fingers break the body in two. Darkness trebles light waning bees. My styrofoam anxiety a cup misplaced I bite into moons. Print-crescents. Your foot on soil as proof of where sadness went. Why I didn't have reason to change my mind, pick each wild iris apart. I see you not. Your foot shores my other. This pattern to sea pebbles larger notions of stability. Sodden bread spreads where we left it. Your arm confused with mine. The envy of sands, rocks war up.

Reading Skin

The first part I can smell. Collagen gem, you remove yourself loyally. Elastic with each tense. You agree to connect black swells. Little orange heads where warmth was. No fissures but self-made one millimeter thick. You resist violences. Water stains, microbes, heat. A rhythmic weight veins spider through. A turnover eye widening and yet you don't abandon line by line. Unafraid, you stretch marks to adjust and slough fingerprints off. You as in any one interrupted only by hair. Exposed to failure, you become thicker, defensive. Your cells increase at your deepest layers. Beneath, tensile strength called a hide. What is hidden by soap and air.

Inside the Construction

Inside my skin are patterns of others' skin. A terminal, branching compass. A number I am supposed to take. Here, raw eggs replace the sun. Parched eyes, bloodshot holes where mouths should be. Nothing believable because all rends further in : Weathered veins circle ancillary. Even they feel observed under bruised elasticity, seven layers deep. They color what's seen : People become bobbed heads. August buoys in mossy lakes. Sightless motors in cotton wind. What belongs and what has real entrance? In the center of the house, I pile roadside pebbles, campground seashells. They reflect themselves. I cancel my experience by describing it. Cracked bridles' acrid lack. Sun spokes or yolks spin out to greener pastures. The ground isn't soft and there aren't orange flowers. Nothing gained, I return the stones. Draw the number. Dump the carapace. Grin and cast these over shoulder-grimace because salty role play only tickles wounds. Doors unhinge. Slap story backing. Pinch beneath. The largest organ dissolves. Soil, too, determines from the inside out.

Writing the Geography

A silver that adds archway. To walk between this day and the next. The sun will rear above the black beach, the long sea. Mark what warms or burns. What questions. If we are honest as any treeless place, the stones resemble ellipses losing balance. He says I'm sorry I narrate everyone I meet. I misread this shore to be a paragraph, a story arc to sail through catharsis. I draw one line across the sand, and then you are a shadow, a body walking the horizon.

Domestics

Perimeters make a place : popcorn kernels you leave in the
doorway where shoes collect cracked leather. Unknown
dander laces the eyelet of my mouth. In lamplight, a
used sponge our agate blackens. I attempt to translate
each part. The Chinese fortune you pick from a yellow
street weed. You claim there's more agency in a thing
left untouched for so long. As if, looking through it, a
water glass curves lamp glow or measures a piano leg's
strength. To fix diameter, I count plants and stack books
in each corner of the room. The plants grow in dirt where
rocks were. Water grows in your voice. All around mine.
I build an invariable. Fold between bed and white linen.
Afternoon is late and fogs glass but promises to return
nothing. Zippers click dryer hum. Shower steam recalls
places you've been in the way mist hits air. The faucet
will someday outrun us. You stuff the fortune in plastic
to preserve it.

How we actually remember

Trauma is the interruption of a feeling before it's
completed. As when smoke curls into narration coloring
air with ash. Memory projects what could not be and
what we thirst. Do we remember wrong? Milkweed
blackens sky or gathers wind. Certain words—lilac,
thrum, bluster, chair, forget—they spread in slow
motion and keep us waiting. With such borrowed
words we want structured sentences, as if a sentence
within these soundproof walls could open chaos. If
this limpid spring could remind us of lightning or the
faces we cut into stars, if we never modified the past
with our present, would emotion be a means by which
to measure truth?

Truss Bridge

A framework composed of individuals. The cairn outside our steps where sand attracts itself. Two parts fastened so tight that overloaded, joints produce only direct tension. You, I, and the your between. A triangle as the only geometric figure that changes form when you lengthen its sides. Surprise draws crescents under arms : one pine branch snaps back the unexpectedly. In its simplest form, every truss is a triangle. You kneel supine actually the sweat transpires my neckline. Truss members are pinned together or their plates are riveted. Tongue-white and salty, your breath dries what we see. The bridge consists of two vertical trusses that carry the floor and the load. Your heels bare now unscab their peels and the cracked ground also. In the planes of the top and bottom cords, two horizontal trusses carry a horizontal wind load. Even windsilk I run against chases more wind. The end posts called portals and the intermediate called sway bracing. I insist your finger stutters mine. Together, the main ties, hip verticals, counters, and posts are called "webs." Unworthy you said sunlight diffuses ocean lowing sea-static, merges one and then the other.

Rituals are obligations so you learn how to grieve

Reykjavik

Back slap whiskey singes, demands them. As if you reach to unload schooner barrels of herring, cod, trout. Salt air callouses red brine. Lungs burn. You load and unload the vessel because you too are a vessel defined by water in which you grew and in which you now grow. Because without them there is no way to forget. Because the village's dusty crossing outlines the future. Repetition of palm to fish and hand to mouth.

Taxi Driver

Rio

Avenida Antlantico, Copacabana at dusk. As in, everyone needs a place to go. Black coffee between my legs, orange rinds at my feet. My throat swollen from kerosene roadsides, sewer mist, clotheslines' horizon hem. One white dress billows the bowl of night. It is easier to long for silence than to live in it. So I drive yolk fed lamplight, shutter summerlong alleys. Tomorrow, I will drive into dilated noon. One eye twitching its solitary way. Words caw and rub against day's end. If you were here I would say I wanted to be involuntary. My tongue pressed to the back of my mouth.

City to Country

Inside a car, sun-clenched thought you take
back. I untends you. Rain in the nearer. Ruins
rinse, and it pleases, though you do regret
leaving skybones' scraping drone. *This is
real.* River white tusking unbraids the thick
word awash. We follow like the edge of bread.
Laziness hums wet tire rub and forgets. Rituals
I watch you seat strangely and I want them.
Lipstick smears the sunset's rearview. Yawn of
grass and fern. Dripping leaves needle maple
distances. The odometer we deny looking
would admit the fear of open spaces. *You* are
flushed out to believe you won't fall from here.
Reeds flee. Mud cliffs so wet the hillside's on
its knees.

Rituals are obligations so you learn how to speak

Sao Paulo

As in an aquarium, water surrounds every accent a glass I
shatter with trying. My fingers heaving arms held akimbo.
City streets so loud at dusk every noise a lipped vowel. Child
venders sell comics to donkey pinatas. Red sunglasses throw
roasted peanuts. Three women on the corner trade God
for popcorn. Sky falls inside my mind, blistered with stars
I can't see. I want to cradle *rua* and *sampa* and *obrigatto,*
but how can you hold shapes or the songs inside? A body
inside a body inside a body. Taxis click past Avenue Paulista.
Yellow bleats litter to taste a warm slow open. A melon
sliced in two.

We must imagine Sisyphus happy

Follow your shadow to determine where to go. A sun ladder falls chromatically. Scale your will, feet first. A stretching of nature or nurture still to be proven in the gathering of moss and heather. In the breach position, what could yield with the help of wheels. Repelling off sky, or some substitute for. As the hero, your eyes and ears that must fill. Scrap metal and fog. Your rock still yours, unblemished by daybreak or what can't be broken. What lives inside your breath rising openly over the harbor, your mother tongue of crushed snails and dried grass. Snap a twig. Expectations once dismembered shall dismember. Face to rock, rock to mud, words to piles now a cairn panting in the history of unopenings. Always waiting for a breathing space, for light about to arrive. Your head rests on your boulder, never growing older, counting back the numbers between 0 and 1.

Fiction, I

All lakes are oceans, all land is sea.
Cause and effect and cause. Water's
cyclic movements. Salt inside a shell,
inside a body, inside a cell. A sign is
a block, an island, a cloud, a clock. A
reference to ocean suspended in rain.
Evaporation as story, no straight lines.
What we can't see still hovers as late
storms. There is a V and there is an A,
and these are thwarted.

My Aegisthus

You seduced her to shut me out. A lisping at your bare feet
until lips strip and ruin. Pine top splay pointing, pine guilt
spreads needles splintering glass. Your eyes strain forest dust
and bend. This stone broken by sand. These eyes fissured by
bones. A dumb blue jay echoes muter near our house, where
bricks crush plumage raw. *Thhh* his feathered wind. What?
Father, you choose never, until, or anyone. A blood forest
answers only with blood. Her veins collect lines in this red
light. Inside, her inner orchard wilts your slate that promises
lies but grows not. Darker underground, sag the fat wet fruit
you thrust. Into my mouth, stuff those fallen needles and husk
my cotton flowering. *Thhh* a blue jay sings. Who buried whom
and what died first? Until a seed of gooseflesh digs bright into
hers or mine or yours, sing from all gardens outside your coffin
of a sometimes grief.

Near Krafla Volcano, Iceland

Canyon yawn roots wheat, maybe cattails.
River encroaches northward, tips almost
nothing; fields grow sky. Believes landscapes
tortured, breached and breaching. We feel.
Water boils under feet, frost grounds red
tidal waves' torsion. Small thuds beneath.
Shoes so superficial, thinks lava magma but
thinks nothing honestly.

The retina focuses only on change

Winter dots in motion. I won't see what you do. A lamppost of black birds flaps a feather ladder. One wing shrugs into sun-flinch. Survival in context as the reason for memory, I mistake your finger for mine. The fire hydrant for fire. Because periphery only believes in movement, city snow ticks us through signaled streets. Power lines thicken tulle fog. Colors appear but we only see in black and white first. The perfidy of an oil blackened road. If I leave now, the eye-sized chink in our windshield. What upturns a juniper's claw at the expense of a snowplow. Because the brain is always goal directed, my distance already charted in ice buried mustard flowers. A cirrus network of scars. The sun jostles our small frames into pins of light that mesh inside the window. What would widen and split.

Bending to

Rain stutter, hesitation of leaves. Rain sheets whitened by sky's contrast. City, skylines turned pulp in fog, and the sudden question of entrance. To be astonished, we become mirrors resting inside freeway spines, our desire hidden inside the sound of wheels. Cement vertigo. The no inside alone. What color is an answer, with eyes edged coal, stomach of soured reds. What slopes inside vowel belly, rounded O and i is engulfed, still *another*—Where does the *we* go from here—even stitches recede to mere balding. Soon curtained moon, a fingernail pressed to fingertipped stars, a point to diameter beyond sea. Blue tissue folds skywards, in its blown weight. You must break it to use it.

at the yield point : in the way of harbors

Any increase in the stress beyond the yield point causes greater permanent deformation and eventually, fracture.

The Last Word

why don't you say something / nice for once / the baby rattle snakes back / and

forth on the cheerio / crumbs flailing the car / floor we should get over / green

grass that hurts / and moves on the railroad / tracks open the mountain / in

two parts / with a hole always / at the center / we hold our breath / then exhale

waiting / for the moon to arrive / in one piece / we force / to feel / relief at the

rumble / strip aching / its dark sounding / its small siren / in gravel warning /

like sandpaper tasted / suddenly under / the tongue chalking teeth / forth and

back to no / reason we tether / for the last word / our baby bobbing / the car

seat / like a sad animal / I'll count to ten / you'll count on swallowing / my back

and forth / how many times / you apologize I / become an echo / a hollow /

a hollow who / I really wish / was sorry

A Body Maps

We drive glacial river bridged   north, not west—Arctic sea. Strange, to think
estuary flows—   water becomes ice, water becomes salt, water becomes
mine. He talks to map polarities; volcanic boil   thaws snow-muddied
crossroads, soil stilted.   Whitened   needs almost blinded rain-
wash, blue-fielded mosses actually blue morning light gazes evening.
                    No noon, no such absolutes, sun-tricks. He speaks
of *our* farm where rented sleep hay scratched thick roughage, no sheets on our
bed. It's warm for February black coffee, boiled fish heads, Island folk records
static radio, and night
drops snow stilled tractors.

                A land abandons itself every season.

Frost tills yellows, hillsides; it's really no different here :

Fjords open like envelopes rip across each shaking finger—he points, afraid—
the tip of the world.

To Be Invisible

I admit little deaths.

City lung-shards   pulp cigarettes.

Dust, zero aperture.

So the causeway imitates   the dial of weathervanes.

My red-combed sweeping.

Eyes as the reason   we can't see, I toss

the seed into the river.

As if a penny can turn itself.   In a palm,

gleaming. I become

an albeit.   A black cat licks

his eye-whites clean.

A gibbet moon   banana ugly.

Cyclone metal

guns skeletal   and fences nothing.

Smaller, my whine pines

the taste of mud.

A tractor bleats   diesel rattle

and so we list ourselves.

Ribbed fern sway   mistakes breathing.

No returns, a hinge

clamps each shutter   I shiver back.

In the garden, a woman

stuffs her mouth with quarters   to count them.

I swallow to watch her.

Every Figure 1 : I

: is concentric :

: rakes sand to remove pine needles :

: believes in the impersonal :

: melts ice left in the glass :

: sees story arc in oceans :

: writes down what's eaten :

: differentiates :

: mistakes highway tire treads for dead crows :

: grows in sand :

: chalks a nightstand with aspirin :

: can reply, "The tumbleweed barbs the rumble strip hills" :

: is damp :

: thinks the heart has a smell :

: believes the deer will migrate through the deer underpass and live

    into the other side :

: is a member :

: will argue, "Mushrooms and stones are currency." :

: slips :

: collects green bottles to empty them :

: can't see her full body when looking directly :

: is why :

: believes the river has a beginning :

: will pay for it :

You must build a new bridge
before demolishing the old one

portland cement / sand in a small town / as any you're a

crane / you're several tractors a story enlists /

infrastructure as in caterpillar / you need names for

what   allows people / crushed rock and water / to

move one space to another /   men and one woman /

in orange cones / warn what's coming / orange / what's

taken away /   say what scars a tractor / what claws a

metal's beating to back up screeching / concrete when

we fall / accidental /   say the blackboard is a road /

for walking /

                                        the wet smell of tar

you need the small / shown from stone / you need an

optical /   waterfall illusion /   your hunched

body /   dressed in milk / cartons left the river's

edge

                  use a galvanized pail / water / twisting

itself white / and brown at the neck / combine aggregates

freed / from all organic material / faucet ripples

                                    voice notions

you collect trusses / always iron X's climb horizontal

ladders / a crane made of triangles / blue jays confuse

     with trees /   rare silence

          full of itself / river glass

cracks / effortless white tusks /   in your error /

measure honest use / four cables hold

          down / the hook

yellow-heavy /   / one side will be higher / than

the other /

     poppy matchsticks /

          wind lit wind

The Day Before the Burial

Sky glare off the road, I get up without / saying. Dust and parakeets cage the isles / tremble the toilet. This is California. Vine rows muffle / with bright they begin early because it's hot in July. Center divide raw in the wheels' way. Wide yawn steers spokes / but speak not of her turning / they have to bury her quickly. Two hornets buzz the skylight. Hum against sleepiness, against. / Enter the room and / metal chairs. Two cross-shaped horses. / A closed casket closes / emerald her eye ended as if taped with granite / stones   *No I don't want to see her*, I said. Reddish complexion coffee with milk gestures I'm not sure she made / Night air fills lilacs, a soon darkness / rustles the back room. Some shiny screws not screwed down / all the way. / An idea of knitting / in the pines, rivers in her face / twists in her mouth broken / veins in the pines. Rivers drool her mouth spittle unknowing afraid. / I said, *I don't want to see her but it doesn't mean / anything* a flat bandage where her nose / was an audience of eyes floating on chairs. / My Marlboro fume escapes / their clothes and how I can't hear / apron strings. Tie their hearts bulging out / fists take up space. Float hot lilacs shining some screws in a chair. One hornet buzzes the / skylight's broken veins in the vines. Broken rivers in my face / knitting my fist. It's like that for them / rustling / in the backroom, California. / It's all or nothing.

Before Fracture

: you wanted the hotel window :

: because the chandelier of your mind has gone out :

: across the power lines :

: the formwork must not be removed for 36 hours :

: with one hand :

: a city rents your heart :

: because you wanted the hotel window to look : to the street :

: concrete is deposited in such : a manner as will prevent the

    separation of ingredients :

: I crossed out :

: to whisper at the size of it :

: back lawn scatters lint under the clothesline :

: the concrete lot :

: so reason evacuates :

: the chandelier of your mind :

: where we count dimples in the concrete lot of where :

: care must be taken : to insure the coating : metal with mortar : a

    thorough compacting :

: obsession for what one can : hold with one hand :

: in the robin's throat : opening across the power : lines shining parallel :

: distance we spare : tired eyes for change :

: the lose : lose of midnight :

: the o of your smile :

: bullet-pointing us :

A Body Maps

                                        World opened, afraid points
                        he
finger shaking tips across ripped fjords :
                        Differences are hillsides; yellow tills frost.
            Seasons abandon land.
                                        A tractor stills snow, drops
night and radio static. Records island. Head fishes boiled coffee, black
    February. Warmth
beds *our* sheets, no, roughage rents scratched hay-sleep. Farms our speak
    tricks.
Sun's absolute noons no evening.
                                        Morning gazes light blue,
mosses wash fielded rain. Blinded needs almost   whitened.
        Stilted soil's crossroads, muddied-snow thaw   boils. Volcanic
    polarities
map talk. He mines water, becomes salt, becomes water, becomes   flows.
    Estuary thinks to strange sea, arctic west. Not north   bridged river, glacial
    drives *we*

Without Duration

: wind trumpets : my hair

splays : the tulip of

my body : swarms

morning : milky noon

absolutes : gather

friction : rattle away

expectation : for you

slips : unposed

breast : drips our

gusted arms : to defend

nakedness : unpeel

skin : breath : peering

your eye : to open :

mine and this : moment

never : to return

anguish : runs

against against :

I now a merely—

broken circuit

seeking : what flees

water : what mothers

a cirrus : blown

back : to what is

: a floating circus :

in sight of : unbroken

sun anchored : by sound

feeling : ungathers

without : pause : without

every I : I face

off suddenly :

arching : your

internal brow now

awakes floating

breath : confides

a sea : to foam

us : a water

psalm : against

denial :

against : the body

dashing itself

Triangulation

/ we washed ourselves and every blanket / I found the night / visit /
prancing the side of your ear / consequence of a road / swollen with
pavers / your eyes drier / from generated heat / fears when you
fell / your grandmother didn't / rush for ice / but at me at stones
/ steadied by / stones your smile didn't end / blame / or our old
pyramids rebuilding / all the glass tables / in her house / we return
/ so the side of your head / rearranged us / and our cat's body / as
even the most docile / human animal wishes / to own / freedom /
in your infancy I / read all pets are an effect / to count on disowning
/ we're all / temporary / a constellation / mind

Reconstruction : *Christchurch, New Zealand*

we go inside to look for damage

in cracked sheer walls buckled high beams

without much light / we wander / lanes visibly

leaning and partially collapsed / The Grand Chancellor /

precariously steadied by neighborhood buildings

/ we perform / emergency / reassessments particularly for

movement must be guided / by what is

heaviest / I feel each sticker to label

trauma green, yellow, or red / surfaces

categorize / the firemen standing over parapets fallen

gargoyles decimated facades shatter

skylight / shadows longer now / everywhere

aftershocks / four times a day or the possibility

of joy thickens bricks bricks bricks on streets

/ we're told were cleared / of dead pigeons

drying / squashed toads / in summer heat

you can't enter / a red building / or anything

/ opening so / without a charter to grant

a search warrant for the ten-story / tenfold /

wreckage in the lobby café gathering safety

glass around tables abandoned / islands harbor

half eaten bacon and eggs rotting / the urban rescue /

debris away from / cell phones lost

to their own rings still piling hasty

overgreased basements flooding a blue glow

/ muddy water / floats through the unsold

TV sets from the 70s storage unit

/ we count / how many seismologists it takes

to fail what substantially broken

/ or free of severe injury / can really mean

to measure the number of cracked wineglass-

claws green bottle rims searing / our

demand for a lifeline / water and power

/ systems wired / into sewer nests of black sludge

and CPR dummies where our / *our* / can't collapse

or at least not everyone will get out

/ alive /

Kin

four men

hold you

/ down /   when night

is not the only night

your upspeak

heavy-lidded

/

underwater

four walls breach

a payphone

/ hanging /

ring upon ring

most promises   /   break

on hello

your window
clacks / tree-bones
branching back winter
        /   and the
                        winter in your head

                        you return always here
                        a kind of / bending
                            flat sheet halo /

swaying
flat / nurse's voice   / yellows your naked /
backed sun
bares its dirty bulb

with sunlight you remain
obsessed
with / what /   ties or
spills

wanting to crawl
                open
        /   within
one silver thread

one orb
rises with / leaning
but
must return

                    /
              darkness
                      hangs
              / your eye /
                    /
              melts wax

insistence
lulls your bed
empties
wings
          / always /
where / lit is

              steering fieldless
                    one   hand on

                              / the moon /
                              one hand off
                              /   /

                              knuckled
                                sky

The passion caused by the great and sublime in nature [. . .] is Astonishment; and astonishment is that state of the soul, in which all its motions are suspended, with some degree of horror. In this case the mind is so entirely filled with its object, that it cannot entertain any other

—Edmond Burke, *On the Sublime*

/ Dilation /

sight returns / impossibility

now a country

of where / we'll never
see /

/ swimming you emerge /

forty weeks under /
screaming in a stranger / palm reading
your first body / *How*

will I know it's you? / when holding

limbs that grew

from holding / what /
I
let go of / sleep   the humidifier

I flood to force

song /

lean out

the unsung /   wilderness   in some

prelude

to / terrible

/ untended

/ joy /

Inside the sound of the mind's hotel

if only a city
sounding the sea breaking
/ a shore

if only
sound
could open   /   winter
rattling what's emptied

a city staggers
gold trembles rimming
all little white lies

it takes one
/
two
and then there's the
city

a radio tallows its oily harbor
its pebbly lists good /
        bargains fester
nesting gull chatter

               in what's dirtiest
                   a twist of tar

turbulence   salts a smile
    date palms clack
        an eye

           a hummingbird's dark / thrums
               a winged frenzy

if I heard
                me
        here
                sounding shores breaking
lazy sea hum moors / traffic cars
        in the bathroom light left on
        to avoid thinking

                tire treads peel
                static / off the rumble
                strip /   mimic now the absent
                        rain

                                        if only the itch of pebbles

                    in my eyes / the gravel
                    in my voice

sound scrapes out the pink
of my mouth / the roof
                        of us

Waiting

after Elizabeth Bishop

I
   keep

      winter /

               /   inside
                   a long time

            I

                              /

                   spill   /

                   rivulets

dress

            a dead wound

                              /   string

         light

            horrifying

right through to

/

/

cover

/ margins

An OH!

I might have been

/

completely

in my mouth

without

falling

to the

room

grown

/   inside

time

/

I said

you'll be

/ to stop /

falling off the turning /

blue-black

I felt :   an I

/ of them

to look

to   what it was

I gave

/   /

   shadows   knees

      pairs of hands

         lying / under

                nothing

      that
could ever

                  be

        the family
     /   in my throat

    those hanging

us altogether

   made us   One
/ word /   -how

How   to be here
like
a cry   that could have

             room-bright
     /   sliding

             /

I was

the war   outside/
               in

               night slush

and it was still

                    said

               /   /

81

/ turning /

I felt :

/   /

shadow hands

                                    /

one

/ word /   —how

a cry

that could have

room

Notes

Definitions for "yield point", a structural engineering term, were taken from *A History of the Theory of Elasticity and the Strength of Materials* by Isaac Toddhunter (1886).

Some of the language and engineering definitions in "Truss Bridge", "You must build a new bridge before demolishing the old one", "Inside the Construction,", "Reconstruction: Christchurch", and "Before Fracture" were adapted from *Structural Engineer's Handbook: Data for the Design and Construction of Steel Bridges And Buildings* (Third Edition, 1941) by Milo S. Ketchum (original copyright, 1914).

"The Day Before the Burial" adapts some of its language from the first section of Camus' *L'Étranger.*

I consulted *Skin: A Natural History* (Nina Jablonski) while writing "Reading Skin."

A few of the poems in *these threads a sound* respond to Arthur Rimbaud's *Les Illuminations*, from *Arthur Rimbaud: Oeuvres complète*, éditions Gallimard (1972).

"Without Duration" is dedicated to Naf Tali, with inspiration from Fernando Pessoa's *The Book of Disquiet.*

This book is dedicated to unpublished poet, grandmother, and California farmer/business owner Ethel A. Telfer (1919-2004). This book is also dedicated to my former student, Jackie Wong, who chose to leave this world in 2011.

With deep gratitude to my partner, Owen Rosenboom, for generously giving me the support and space I needed to draft and revise these poems.

With infinite thanks as well to those who gave me vital feedback and encouragement during the drafting process of these poems, including Tiff Dressen, Shamala Gallagher, Rob Halpern, Raina J. León, Rusty Morrison, Aaron Shurin, Kevin Simmonds, Ed Smallfield, Valerie Witte, and Annie Won.

small siren was printed in an edition of 250 copies
on Glatfelter 55# Natural Offset Antique
by McNaughton & Gunn

Text was set in Questa

Design by Jon Grizzle
Photograph by Adam Thorman